MASTERING THE ART OF STRATEGIC THINKING:

DEVELOPING A STRATEGIC MINDSET FOR SUCCESS

CARSON BOND. PH.D.

TABLE OF CONTENTS

WHAT IS STRATEGIC THINKING?

Strategic thinking is a deliberate and rational thought process that aims to analyze the important factors and variables that influence the long-term success of a company, group, or individual. Strategic thinking involves guarding against threats and vulnerabilities and carefully anticipating opportunities to pursue them. Such thinking must take into account economic realities, market forces, and available resources.

Strategic thinking requires research, analytical thinking, innovation, problem-solving, communication and leadership skills, and determination. Why is strategic thinking important?

The competitive landscape of any organization can change rapidly.

New trends can emerge quickly and must be taken advantage of or left behind, By incorporating strategic thinking into your daily work and everyday life, you can better anticipate and take advantage of opportunities. Thinking strategically at a personal level can help you prove that you're willing to contribute more to your role, become more critical to the organization, and absorb more resources.

WHAT IS STRATEGIC THINKING IN BUSINESS?

During an organization's annual strategic planning process, leaders often collect, analyze, and synthesize external and internal data and ideas to develop a strategic intent and create a strategic narrative. This document guides the company in the future. Leaders then select and plan specific actions that will achieve these strategic initiatives. Businesses should also schedule time throughout the year for strategic thinking and evaluation. The leadership team should regularly review strategic initiatives to implement, review and sustain efforts across the organization. What is strategic thinking in leadership?

Business leaders and stakeholders use strategic thinking and analysis to determine what product mix to offer, the competitive landscape to compete against, and how to allocate scarce resources such as time, labour, and capital.

They must decide how to properly organize the registration of others in order to achieve important goals and avoid unnecessary waste of resources.

WHAT ARE THE COMPONENTS OF STRATEGIC THINKING?

The company's strategic activity includes analysis, problem solving, decision making and change leadership.

When developing a direction or strategic plan, consider:

- Business opportunities and vulnerabilities

- Possible from any thought or danger

- Expenses associated with the contemplated move.

- The likelihood that other tactics will be effective.

- How to align goals with the overall plan

- The potential impact of competitors, suppliers, customers and new substitutes on strategic planning.

If you identify obstacles in the planning process, address them as follows:

• Gather relevant information about the problem.

• Clearly define the problem from a strategic perspective.

• Brainstorm solutions

• Imagine several challenges and how to overcome them.

• Delegate work on multiple parts of this strategy to key partners.

Strategic thinking requires agility and determination to choose and stick to a plan. However, you should be aware of promising new opportunities. It is an act of finding a balance between consistency and flexibility. You and your team:

• Make sure decisions are well supported by sound research.

• Select goals and related values

• Prioritize your goals

• Follow standard decision-making processes.

• Consensus building where necessary

During strategic planning, you should discuss ideas with your employees and gather feedback. Then use effective channels to communicate a solid picture of the completed plan to all employees and focus on their contributions to the plan.

HOW TO IMPROVE STRATEGIC THINKING TECHNOLOGY

There are five steps to improve strategic thinking technology:

1) Determine the future, give planning, identification and trend, ensure and determine the future to implement resources.

2) Open your opinion so you can think more clearly about the strategy

3) In strategic thinking, you can get opinions from high quality experts in the organization.

4) Find out how to ask a good question: Find out how to find a question like "this idea is the source of information" and "is this logical idea?"

5) Explore all the results of the different strategies and the results of the guidelines.

WHAT IS STRATEGIC THINKING IN LEADERSHIP?

Strategic thinking is a long-term thinking process to achieve a successful team or company. It means predictability, the discipline to prepare now and the ability to position yourself to compete and win in the future. New leaders at all levels must pool resources and energy and focus on priorities that will ensure future business success and growth. The challenge facing strategic leaders is that society as a whole is addicted to short-term thinking.

Day-to-day behaviour puts leaders in a very tactical frame of mind. You worry about managing your to-do list, meeting short-term goals, and meeting today's production schedule. When sales drop, we respond with short-term solutions.

They ignore opportunities to see their situation strategically.

Often they focus on overcoming the current crisis and managing the needs of the day at the expense of the future.

Strategic thinking in leadership is the ability to analyze and understand the big picture of a team or project, anticipate potential challenges and opportunities, and make informed decisions that align with long-term goals. This includes considering the short- and long-term consequences of decisions, prioritizing tasks and projects, and quickly adapting to market or industry changes. Leaders who think strategically can effectively communicate their vision and goals to teams and make data-driven decisions that drive team success.

It should be noted that this skill involves analytical and creative thinking. Leaders who think strategically must be able to collect and analyze data, identify trends and patterns, and use this information to make informed decisions. However, they must be able to think creatively, consider different perspectives and approaches to a problem, and develop solutions that advance the team.

Another important aspect of strategic thinking in leadership is the ability to anticipate change and prepare for the future. This includes developing contingency plans to address potential problems and exploit new opportunities.

WHY IS STRATEGIC THINKING IMPORTANT FOR LEADERS?

When leaders can consider strategic thinking, they have an important skill. They can learn to reason, learn and make decisions to handle unfamiliar situations and enable employees to continue working despite setbacks.

Wherever you are, it's never too late to think and act strategically.

The following elements of strategic thinking can be used as individual skills or combined to create a powerful strategic thinking process:

1. TAKE THE TIME TO PLAN AHEAD

When leaders have time to plan ahead, they are better able to think ahead to their team's long-term goals. This means taking time to think about the future. Routine activities that take up a leader's time are not bad, In fact, it is very important for business continuity. Most importantly, leaders need to set clear boundaries and spend time thinking strategically.

2. LOOKING AT BUSINESS GOALS FROM A DIFFERENT PERSPECTIVE

Changing your perspective can help you better understand your company's real competitive advantage. This requires strategic leadership to optimize investments of time, energy and resources. You can create strategic dashboards to identify strong strategic goals.

3. THE CONTINUOUS COLLECTION OF INTELLIGENCE DATA

As a leader, it is essential to find reliable sources to gather information from blogs, reviews or the internal web. This important activity allows leaders to understand the changes in the business world. Leaders must identify reliable sources of data, be willing to review learning process, and draw conclusions about patterns they discover in the market and in competitors.

4. ADVERSARY FORCE ANALYSIS, SCENARIO FORECASTING, PLANNING AND PROGRESS

The opposing force is the force between your present and future success. By thinking about how to think strategically as a leader, you can better understand and use the power that works to your advantage. Then wait for the future scenario and create a scenario and imagine -how the situation can open in the future. This information is used to plant actions and jumper.

WHAT IS THE ROLE OF STRATEGIC THINKING IN LEADERSHIP AND HOW TO CULTIVATE IT?

Leadership is more than managing people and resources. It is about predicting the future and making plans to achieve it. This is where strategic thinking comes in. Strategic thinking means seeing the big picture, understanding how different parts of a team or project fit together, and making decisions that lead to long-term goals.

Why is strategic thinking important in leadership? Strategic thinking is essential in leadership because it helps you solve problems in your role and drive the success of your team. It's simple to become mired in the minute details while beginning a new leadership position and to lose sight of the bigger vision.

However, by taking a strategic approach, the new leader can set a clear direction for the team and ensure that everyone is working towards a common goal.

One of the key benefits of strategic thinking for new leaders is that it provides a road map to success. As a result, leaders can prioritize tasks and allocate resources efficiently by setting long-term goals and identifying the steps necessary to achieve them. New leaders can foresee and prepare for change thanks to strategic thinking, which is another advantage.

The industry is constantly evolving, and new leaders must adapt to new challenges and opportunities. Leaders that use strategic thinking are better able to recognize potential dangers and opportunities and have backup plans to deal with them.. Finally, strategic thinking in leadership is essential to effective communication. New leaders must be able to effectively, succinctly, and persuasively convey their vision and goals to teams and stakeholders. Strategic thinking helps leaders identify the key messages they need to convey and adapt their communication styles to different stakeholders.

WHAT OTHER STRATEGIC THINKING SKILLS ARE THERE?

Strategic thinking skills include analyzing complex situations, identifying opportunities and challenges, and developing effective strategies to achieve specific goals. This includes critical and creative thinking, considering multiple perspectives and making decisions. Strategic thinking in leadership requires a combination of the following skills:

1. ANALYTICAL SKILLS:

Strategic thinking involves collecting and analyzing data, identifying patterns and trends, and using this information to make decisions. Strategic thinking leaders must be able to interpret complex data sets and gain meaningful insights.

2. COMMUNICATION SKILLS:

Strategic thinking requires the ability to communicate effectively. Leaders who think strategically must communicate their vision and goals clearly, concisely and persuasively to teams and stakeholders. You must also be able to actively listen to the team and provide feedback.

3. PROBLEM-SOLVING SKILLS:

Strategic thinking requires the ability to identify and solve problems. Strategic thinking leaders must be able to look at problems from multiple angles and develop creative solutions that address the root causes of problems.

4. PLANNING AND MANAGEMENT SKILLS:

Strategic thinking involves setting long-term goals and identifying necessary steps. Leaders who think strategically must have the ability to develop and execute strategic plans, allocate resources effectively, and manage risks and opportunities.

HOW TO DEVELOP STRATEGIC THINKING SKILLS?

Strategic thinking in leadership is a skill that is not for everyone, but can be improved with practice.

Here are some tips to improve your strategic thinking skills:

- **INTELLIGENCE GATHERING**:

To think strategically, leaders must have a deep understanding of their team, mission, values, and goals. Managers also need to keep abreast of the latest industry trends, market changes and new technologies. • Data Analytics: Use data to make informed decisions. Analyze patterns, trends, and data to make predictions about the future

- **BE IMAGINATIVE:**

Be fearless and innovative; think about several angles and strategies for tackling issues and challenges.

- **CREATE A PLAN:**

After gathering information and analyzing data, create a plan that aligns with your team's goals and values.

- **ASSESS PROGRESS**:

Regularly review progress toward goals and adjust plans as needed.

Celebrate your accomplishments and take lessons from your mistakes.

HOW CAN MANAGERS IMPROVE THEIR STRATEGIC THINKING SKILLS?

- **ASKING STRATEGIC QUESTIONS:**
Asking the right questions is the key to strategic thinking. Asking open-ended questions that challenge assumptions and reveal new perspectives can help you better understand a problem or opportunity. You can generate original solutions and pinpoint core issues by asking strategic questions that take into account various viewpoints.

• OBSERVE AND REFLECT:

Observing and reflecting on the environment can help develop strategic thinking skills. You can identify growth opportunities and potential risks by analyzing trends and patterns in your industry or market. Reflection allows us to think deeply about our experiences and learn from them, which helps us make informed decisions.

• THINK ABOUT CONTRASTING AND NUMEROUS PERSPECTIVES:

Strategic leadership thinking entails taking into account a range of viewpoints and concepts.

By questioning their presumptions and aggressively seeking out opposing ideas, leaders can broaden their thinking. This allows you to create more reliable strategies and make informed decisions.

- **USE FORMAL TRAINING:**

You can learn new skills and get fresh perspectives by participating in formal strategic thinking training.

The principles and techniques of strategic thinking can be taught in many courses, seminars, and books. This allows you to keep up with the latest trends and best practices and develop your skills in an organized and methodical way.

•**COLLABORATING WITH OTHERS:**
Collaboration helps leaders develop strategic thinking skills by exposing them to new ideas, we work with people from different backgrounds and experiences to gain new perspectives on challenges and develop innovative solutions.

•**LOOK FOR ROLE MODELS:**

It can be beneficial to strengthen your own strategic thinking abilities by observing those who already possess them.. Find mentors and role models who can provide guidance, advice and feedback, and watch them tackle strategic challenges. You'll be able to do this to strengthen your strategic thinking abilities and build a network of support for when you're navigating leadership jobs.

What skills do leaders demonstrate through strong strategic thinking?

•STRATEGIC FLEXIBILITY:

Leaders that are adept at strategizing are able to respond to new problems and rapidly adjust to changing conditions.

They can anticipate potential obstacles and opportunities and adjust their strategies accordingly.

• FLEXIBILITY TO DEAL WITH PARADOXES:

Effective strategic thinkers have the ability to hold seemingly contradictory ideas in mind and find creative solutions to address them. They embrace complexity and ambiguity and can use it to their advantage.

• CLARITY IN THE MIDST OF AMBIGUITY:

Leaders with strong strategic thinking can overcome ambiguity to make sense of complex information. They can identify the key drivers of change and break them down into clear and concise goals and strategies.

• BIGGER TEAM VISION:

Strategic thinkers can see the big picture and understand the impact of their decisions and actions on the team. Align your strategy with the team's overall mission and vision and collaborate with others to achieve a common goal.

SOME HABITS OF STRATEGIC LEADERS

• STRATEGIC LEADERS ARE DEDICATED TO LIFELONG LEARNING AND PERSONAL DEVELOPMENT:

They look for fresh data, concepts, and viewpoints to incorporate into their work. They prioritize continuous professional development and seek opportunities to expand their skills and knowledge.

• LONG-TERM FOCUS:

Strategic leaders can balance short-term goals with long-term vision. They prioritize initiatives that align with the team's strategic direction and can address even short-term challenges.

- **COLLABORATIVE:**

Strategic leaders understand the value of collaboration and actively seek opportunities to collaborate with others. They can build strong teams and partnerships and use diverse perspectives to drive innovation and achieve common goals.

- **BE OPEN TO INNOVATION:**

Strategic leaders are prepared to take calculated risks in order to produce innovative results. They are receptive to new concepts and methods.

They encourage experimentation and learnings and can quickly adapt to changing market conditions or customer needs.

• **LEAD WITH A PURPOSE:** Strategic leaders are guided by a clear purpose and mission. They can articulate a confident vision for the future and inspire others to help make it a reality. We prioritize ethical behaviour and act with integrity in all interactions.

By developing these habits, strategic leaders can drive innovation, build stronger teams, and achieve long-term success for their teams.

CONCLUSION

Strategic thinking in leadership is essential in today's fast-paced environment. Effective strategy leaders possess a range of analytical, communication, problem-solving, planning and management skills. They can receive formal training to ask strategic questions, observe and think, consider opposing ideas, and improve strategic thinking skills. They also develop habits like continuous learning, long-term focus, collaborative thinking, and embracing innovation. By developing these skills and habits, strategic leaders can guide their teams through uncertainty and change and achieve long-term success. Whether you're a new leader trying to develop your strategic thinking or a seasoned leader trying to refine your vision, the key is to remain flexible and adaptable while prioritizing and focusing on continuous learning and self-improvement. Become a successful strategic leader and help your team grow.

Why is strategic thinking important for leaders?

Strategic thinking is essential for leaders because it enables them to see the big picture and foresee upcoming opportunities and difficulties. They are able to create and implement successful strategies that promote growth and success because it enables them to make well-informed decisions that are in line with the team's vision and goals. Leaders who lack a strategic mindset risk becoming reactive, missing opportunities, or underestimating challenges.

What are leaders' strategic responsibilities?

The direction, resource coordination, and decision-making that support the team's long-term performance are the leaders' strategic responsibilities. They have to have a thorough awareness of the team's internal and external environments, recognize important trends and drivers, and foresee issues and opportunities in the future. This knowledge must be transformed into workable strategies and programs that promote development, innovation, and competitive advantage.

How do leaders cultivate a strategic mindset?

The following are some ways that leaders can develop their strategic thinking:

• Participating in ongoing learning and professional development to stay current with market trends and advancements.

• Getting different viewpoints and advice from co-workers, stakeholders, and specialists to better grasp the problems facing the team.

• Supporting risk-taking and innovative thinking by fostering an experimental and innovative culture.

• Establishing specific objectives and goals in line with the mission and values of the team.

How is leadership enhanced by strategic thinking?

With the help of strategic thinking, leaders can:

• Create a clear vision and direction for the team.

• Locate and seize chances for development and innovation.

• Recognize and lessen potential hazards and difficulties.

www.ingramcontent.com/pod-product-compliance
Lightning Source LLC
Chambersburg PA
CBHW072152230526
45467CB00042B/1831

9798392237500